The Salem
Witchcraft
Delusion

In 1692, Massachusetts was a colony beset by many doubts and difficulties and made recently conscious of the devil and his works by two books written by clergymen, Increase and Cotton Mather. When a group of girls in Salem Village (now Danvers) began to act strangely and their doctor declared them to be bewitched, the uneasiness of the local citizens gave way to panic and hysteria. Unwise handling of the affair and prejudiced courtroom procedures served to inflame public opinion still further, until a small local event became a colony-wide sensation. Twenty persons were killed, fifty-five confessed to being witches, and over one hundred and fifty were in jail before the common sense of a few individuals succeeded in stopping the witchcraft accusations. Eventually, in an act almost unparalleled in the history of witchcraft, a large number of the witch-hunters publicly admitted that they had been wrong. Their candor made the Salem cases a landmark on the road to enlightenment and spelled the beginning of the end for witchcraft trials.

PRINCIPALS

INCREASE MATHER, Puritan clergyman of Massachusetts.

COTTON MATHER, his son, also a clergyman.

SAMUEL PARRIS, minister of the Salem Village church and active in the witchcraft affair.

DEODAT LAWSON, a former clergyman in Salem Village and a participant in some of the early events of the witchcraft affair.

ELIZABETH BOOTH, eighteen
SARAH CHURCHILL, twenty
ELIZABETH HUBBARD, seventeen
MERCY LEWIS, seventeen
ANN PUTNAM, twelve
SUSANNA SHELDON, eighteen
MARY WALCOTT, seventeen
MARY WARREN, twenty
ABIGAIL WILLIAMS, eleven

Salem Village's "afflicted girls," supposedly bewitched.

ANN PUTNAM, SR., mother of young Ann and an active accuser of witches.

JOHN HATHORNE, one of the magistrates who presided at the first examinations of the accused witches.

JONATHAN CORWIN, one of the magistrates presiding at the first examinations, and later a judge at the trials.

BARTHOLOMEW GEDNEY
JOHN RICHARDS
PETER SERGEANT
SAMUEL SEWALL   } Judges who presided at the
WILLIAM STOUGHTON   witchcraft trials.
WAIT WINTHROP

SARAH CLOYSE, jailed for witchcraft but not tried.

ABIGAIL HOBBS, a confessed witch who implicated other persons.

DELIVERANCE HOBBS, a confessed witch who implicated other persons.

WILLIAM HOBBS, jailed for witchcraft but not tried.

SARAH OSBURN, jailed for witchcraft but died before trial.

TITUBA, the Parrises' servant, accused of witchcraft, who in her confession evidenced the scope of the affair.

ELIZABETH PROCTER, convicted of witchcraft but saved from death by reprieve.

BRIDGET BISHOP
GEORGE BURROUGHS
MARTHA CARRIER
MARTHA COREY
MARY ESTY
SARAH GOOD
ELIZABETH HOW
GEORGE JACOBS, SR.
SUSANNA MARTIN
REBECCA NURSE   } Convicted of witchcraft and hanged
ALICE PARKER   on Gallows Hill in Salem in 1692.
MARY PARKER
JOHN PROCTER
ANN PUDEATOR
WILMOT REED
MARGARET SCOTT
SAMUEL WARDWELL
SARAH WILDS
JOHN WILLARD

GILES COREY, accused of witchcraft and pressed to death for defying the court.

SIR WILLIAM PHIPS, royal governor of Massachusetts in 1692.

A FOCUS BOOK

The Salem Witchcraft Delusion, 1692

"Have You Made No Contract with the Devil?"

by Alice Dickinson

Alice (Dickinson) Hoke   pseud.

FRANKLIN WATTS, INC.
NEW YORK / 1974

The authors and publisher of the Focus Books
wish to acknowledge the helpful editorial
suggestions of Professor Richard B. Morris.

Cover by Ginger Giles
Photo research by Selma Hamdan

Photographs courtesy of:
Library of Congress–pp. 12; New York Public
Library Picture Collection–frontis, opp. pp. 1,
pps. 5, 18, 20, 31, 42, 53, 61; U.S. Bureau of
Public Roads–pp. 38.

Library of Congress Cataloging in Publication Data

Dickinson, Alice.
    The Salem witchcraft delusion, 1692.

    (A Focus book)
    Bibliography: p.
    SUMMARY: Discusses the social and religious
climate that led to the Salem witch hunts and
describes the trials and their aftermath.
    1. Witchcraft–Massachusetts–Juvenile litera-
ture. [1. Witchcraft–Massachusetts] I. Title.
BF1576.D5   272'.8   73–12085
ISBN 0–531–01049–X

Contents

A World of
Invisible Beings

"Witchcraft is forbidden by this present assembly to be used in this colony; and the penalty imposed by the authority that we are subject to is death," said a Rhode Island colonial law passed in 1647. The colonies of Massachusetts and Connecticut also had laws against witchcraft, and in 1648 one of the Massachusetts courts suggested appointing witch-finders to watch suspected persons.

New England was not alone in its feeling toward witchcraft. Its inhabitants were only echoing long-established beliefs. These colonies had been settled by people from England. They had brought their ideas from the old country. At the time, witchcraft was an accepted fact of life, punishable by law, in England and on the continent of Europe. There, hundreds of persons were hanged or burned as witches each year.

Today we may think it odd that witches should have been considered so real a danger that laws against them seemed necessary, but we must remember that the world of three centuries ago was still emerging from the dark mysteries and superstitions of the Middle Ages. A belief in witchcraft went back to primitive times. Then, slowly, in the early seventeenth century, science was being born. Copernicus had challenged the age-old image of the earth as the center of the universe when he declared that the planets rotated around the sun, and Galileo had later supported his views. Before the century was over, Isaac Newton and others would open new scientific windows.

This engraving shows various ways in which it was believed the devil could operate.

[1]

For most early seventeenth-century people in the Western world, however, the old ideas still held. The earth was ruled by a powerful, awe-inspiring God, from whom good might flow. But evil was always present, and the Prince of Evil, the devil, lurked near—a very real person although he was invisible—ever ready to ruin those unfortunates who fell under his spell. Good or bad, whatever happened to an individual was thought to be the work either of God or of the devil. There were no natural causes. At a time when thunder and lightning, hurricanes, and disease still were mysteries, people judged them and other natural disasters to be the work of an awful, vengeful, unseen power. Most seventeenth-century human beings felt that they lived surrounded by invisible beings, of whose presence they were always aware.

But there was a general belief that the devil could do no physical harm directly to human beings; he had to act through a go-between—a witch—who had made a personal contract with him. A possible candidate might be approached by the devil himself or by someone who had already become a confederate of his. In exchange for certain powers and favors, the candidate-witch was asked to sign in blood in the devil's book, swearing to worship God no longer but instead to worship the devil. By doing evil and mischief to human beings, she would promote the devil's plans to conquer the earth. Men also might make a contract with the devil and practice witchcraft; they were more commonly known as wizards.

Oaths of allegiance to the devil were usually made at midnight meetings of all the witches and wizards of a district, with the Prince of Evil himself or one of his chief wizards presiding. There, reports of evildoing were made and new mischief was planned. Once the business of a meeting was settled and the new witches had been received, rites that were a mockery of the sacred mass or communion of the church took place. Then came the feasting and dancing and wild orgies that lasted until dawn's first light.

In return for allegiance, the devil granted each witch a "familiar," a spirit who became her companion in evildoing, always ready to do her bidding. The familiar could even take the form of a specter, a phantom assuming the witch's personal appearance and going out from her body, perhaps traveling many miles to pinch and torture a victim while the witch herself stayed innocently at home. The witch was also given phantom familiars in the form of animals. Rats, toads, yellow birds, and spiders were favorites among these.

One of the witch's greatest powers was image magic. By making an image of an enemy out of wax, rags, horsehair, goat's hair, or other materials, she had the victim in her power. If she stuck a pin in the image's head, the real person, although far away, would suffer an unbearable headache. If she tightened her fingers around the image's neck, the real person would surely choke. If she slowly melted a figure of wax, the real person would just as slowly waste away. The possibilities of image mischief were endless.

In the seventeenth century, almost everyone, even the most educated persons, believed in witchcraft and recognized it as an evil. There had been a time when some witches had the reputation for doing good deeds, but the church of the Middle Ages had firmly associated witches with heretics and the devil. Now witches were greatly feared. They could do terrible harm to persons they disliked, and they had special skills. They could read minds, foretell the future, throw awful temptations in the path of the godly, and even raise the ghosts of the dead, who might then reveal never-suspected acts of murder. Once a person had made a contract with the devil, there was only one way to break her power—by killing her. She was brought to trial, and if found guilty by a jury, was put to death. Put in Drawing

Some persons actually practiced witchcraft and it worked —because people in general believed in it so thoroughly. If a person discovered that a witch had been making image magic against him, for instance, he was seized by such terror and such a sense of doom that his life fell apart. A curse from a witch's lips was enough to send a person into a fit of depression and hopelessness that might even bring on death. Merely a look from a supposed witch's evil eye could send a victim into writhings of pain. Then nothing could cure him so readily as a touch of that same witch's hand—because he believed in the evil eye and the witch's touch. Fear has a terrible power.

Some persons, because of their appearance or behavior, were suspected of practicing witchcraft even though they did not. A few of them found it an advantage to encourage this suspicion. Even their most idle threat could then produce such terror that it amounted to blackmail. But these people played a perilous game. Their most casual "The devil take you" or "You'll live to regret this day" might have unforeseen results. Suppose the person they had threatened fell accidentally soon afterward and broke his leg. He would know whom to blame. In a world where people are convinced of witchcraft, nothing is accidental.

People who believed wholeheartedly in witches were always on the lookout for them. As a consequence, many persons were unjustly condemned to death. The poor, the elderly, the cranks, the half-crazed, the rude and quarrelsome—all were natural suspects to witch-hunters. In the old records of witchcraft cases, it is noteworthy how often the accused witch was a poor, elderly person or an ill-tempered hag who fought with her neighbors and threatened them unceasingly, and was blamed for any ill fortune that came their way.

One test for a witch: the accused is tied and thrown into a stream; if she floats she is considered guilty, since it was believed that pure water would reject someone who was impure. If she sank, she was innocent, which might have been little solace to the accused unless she were quickly pulled out of the water.

To seventeenth-century people, witchcraft loomed as a very real danger, always in the background and never quite forgotten. Suspected witches might go unaccused for a long time, but when political, religious, economic, or natural misfortunes struck on a large scale, all the old suspicions were suddenly voiced as people sought the cause of their troubles. The larger outbreaks of witch-hunting have always come when there was some unease among the mass of people. The Salem witchcraft delusion, which took place in the colony of Massachusetts in 1692, was no exception.

The Bible Colony

Massachusetts had been settled by English Puritans. Their religious beliefs had driven them from the established church while they were still living in England. They felt that the church rituals and ceremonies were vain and wicked, and they deplored the corruption of many of the clergymen. Feeling that they needed a more direct communion with God, the Puritans wished to establish themselves in small congregations, each free to choose its own clergyman and worship at a simple service. Instead of belonging to a national church with bishops and other officials in power, each congregation would be independent and would receive its authority directly from God. Persons who joined a congregation would be obliged to satisfy their fellow members that they followed God's word. The members of the Puritan church would be a zealous band of true believers to whom the Bible was the final law in all things, even matters of civil government.

Their desire to "purify" the Church of England and to reform it according to their own ideas brought the Puritans into conflict with church authorities. At last, despairing of gaining their ends in England, some of the Puritans began to make plans for emigrating to New England. There they hoped to set up a colony where they could establish their own church, which they felt was the one true church of God.

In time, the Puritans organized a shareholding stock company. In 1629, they received a royal charter from Charles I, king of England, granting them rights to a large piece of land on Massachusetts Bay. Those Puritans who planned to be the actual colonists were unwilling to leave their charter in the hands of shareholders who would remain in England. Secretly the emigrating Puritans bought up the shares owned by the men who were staying behind, and when they left England they took the charter with them. Now that it was safely in their possession, they felt that they could create their ideal state without any interference from across the seas.

In June, 1630, the Puritans arrived at Salem, which was already settled. John Winthrop was chosen as their governor, and the work of building the new colony began. The colonists settled in towns, each of which had its church and its minister. Those townspeople who were recognized as true believers in God's word were accepted as church members. They could vote in the town meetings. Those settlers who could not satisfy the minister and congregation of their religious faith or who did not care to be questioned about their beliefs were not allowed to join the church. Neither they nor the apprentices and servants of the colony had voting rights.

Since only church members could vote, it followed that the church and the civil government were closely intertwined. The voters, church members themselves, elected only those officials whom they considered godly—other church members. In governing, the town officials took no important step without first consulting the local clergyman. When any doubts arose, the Bible was the final guide on how to proceed. One of the primary duties of the magistrates, or judges, of the courts was to uphold the Puritan religion.

Even private citizens were encouraged to watch their neighbors closely and report to the minister anyone who strayed even slightly from the "straight and narrow." The Puritans firmly believed that God had chosen them for his special care. "Know this is the place where the Lord will create a new Heaven, and a new Earth, in new Churches; and a new Commonwealth together," said Edward Johnson in his book *Wonder-working Providence of Sion's Saviour in New England*, published in 1654. The Puritan church members intended to be worthy of God's trust.

Because they had such supreme confidence that their colony was God's own, the Puritans had no tolerance for persons of differing religious beliefs. Massachusetts was for Puritans only; no others need apply. Roger Williams and Anne Hutchinson found no welcome in Massachusetts when they voiced opinions that seemed heretical to authorities. The Baptists and the Quakers who entered the colony from time to time were cruelly persecuted. Some members of the Church of England eventually settled in Massachusetts, but they were forbidden to worship according to their Book of Common Prayer.

During the early years of the colony, England was in political turmoil and the Puritans received little attention from the mother country; they were free to govern their colony as they thought fitting. But with the death of the Puritan Lord Protector Oliver Cromwell and the restoration of Charles II to the throne of England in 1660, the future of Massachusetts became clouded. In 1664, the king sent a commission to the colony with orders to assert royal power over it. The commissioners were dismayed to see the Puritans' intolerance to persons of differing beliefs. The laws should be changed, they advised the colony's authorities, so that people of other faiths, too, could worship as they felt best.

The idea that Massachusetts should become a home for "heretics" who might convert others to their beliefs was horrifying to the Puritans, who were sure that these people would undermine their Bible colony. But they dared not resist the king's commissioners too far. Resistance might mean the loss of their precious charter, which they considered the foundation of their government. So, gradually, the number of nonbelievers grew, and the solidly Puritan nature of the colony began to change.

Other forces, too, were weakening the Bible colony. A new generation, less religious than the early founders, had grown up. Life was a little easier; as a result, the moral atmosphere was less severe. There was more drunkenness and profanity; more people were breaking the strict rules for conduct on the Sabbath day. Then public calamity struck: King Philip's War in 1675, with its horrible toll of massacre and destruction as Indian and colonist battled; deadly epidemics of disease; a disastrous fire in Boston. In despair at what they saw as the general decay of the colony, the ministers and elders of the churches met in 1679 to discuss "what are the evils that have provoked the Lord to bring his judgments on New England." They concluded that New England would perish unless the people reformed their ways.

But the growing spread of science was fostering a new viewpoint about the causes of events, and the clergymen feared it. At another meeting in 1681, they agreed that the people might be in danger of losing their belief in the existence of invisible spirits of good and evil. In order to rekindle the old-time faith

[9]

of their congregations and remind them of the invisible dangers that always surrounded them, the clergymen decided to collect and publish any accounts they might hear of "such divine tempests, floods, earthquakes, thunders as are unusual, strange apparitions, or whatever else shall happen that is prodigious, witchcrafts, diabolical possessions, remarkable judgments upon noted sinners, eminent deliverances, and answers to prayer."

As a result of this decision, Increase Mather, one of the most eminent clergymen in Massachusetts, published in 1684 *An Essay for the Recording of Illustrious Providences*. Not all the "providences" he recorded were supernatural, but plainly the world of spirits was his real interest. His accounts of New England's witches, poltergeists, hauntings, and persons possessed by the devil set Massachusetts tongues wagging. The colony had been restrained in its treatment of witchcraft, but as people discussed Mather's portrayals of diabolical doings, interest in evil spirits began to grow.

Ever since the royal commissioners' visit in 1664, the Massachusetts authorities had been fighting the English king's demand that they return the colony's charter. The Puritans knew that once the charter was in English hands it would be revised and their complete control over their government would end; the king could do no less than insist that all his subjects be allowed to vote, whether or not they were church members.

The skirmish over the charter was a continuous matching of colonial against royal wits until 1684, when Charles II, in exasperation, ordered the charter revoked. Massachusetts would now become a royal colony with a governor chosen by the king and with voters who were not all Puritan believers. The Puritans could foresee that the old faith on which the colony had been based would be challenged. Perhaps the end of the Bible colony, their ideal state, was near.

The arrival of the royal governor, Sir Edmund Andros, confirmed their worst fears. He ruled like a tyrant. In 1689, the colonists revolted and drove Andros from office. Increase Mather had already gone secretly to England to negotiate a new charter for Massachusetts. With the accession of William and Mary to the throne in 1689, Mather hoped that the original document might be reenacted. William saw the need for a new charter, however; for the time being, Massachusetts remained uncertain about its future government.

The loss of the charter was a hard blow for the Puritans, who were becoming convinced that the devil himself was working against them. What more suitable place was there for him to attack than God's chosen spot on earth? they asked.

The Devil Gains a Toehold

If the Puritans needed further proof of the devil's schemes, they did not have long to wait. In 1689, Cotton Mather, the clergyman son of Increase Mather, published a book called *Memorable Providences relating to Witchcrafts and Possessions*. It was chiefly concerned with a recent case of witchcraft in Boston, involving the children of John Goodwin, a stonemason. When, in 1688, Goodwin's eldest daughter questioned the family's laundress about stealing some linen, the laundress's mother, a Mrs. Glover, "bestowed very bad language" upon the Goodwin girl. Mrs. Glover's husband, before his death, had sometimes said that she was a witch.

Immediately after her encounter with Mrs. Glover, the Goodwin girl began to have strange convulsive seizures. Before long, three more of the Goodwin children were afflicted in the same way. Doctors who were called in decided that "nothing but a hellish witchcraft" could cause such troubles. (Medical science was almost nonexistent at the time, and when doctors were unable to diagnose a difficult case they commonly decided that the patient was bewitched.)

In their affliction, the Goodwin children sometimes were deaf; sometimes they could not speak; sometimes their tongues were drawn down into their throats and at other times hung down at great length upon their chins; at times their jaws were put out of joint and then would clap together like a spring lock. Their bodies sometimes were drawn back into an arch. They cried out because of sharp pains. Their necks would often go limp, then rigid.

Cotton Mather, hearing of the case, had gone to pray with the children. Later, four clergymen of Boston had held a day of prayer for them, and the youngest child recovered.

When the Boston magistrates heard of the case, they hauled Mrs. Glover into court. There she cursed God and could not repeat the Lord's Prayer. (Inability to repeat the prayer was considered almost certain proof that a person was in league with the devil.) When Mrs. Glover's house was searched, some images made of rags were found. At her trial she demonstrated her magic powers. Wetting her finger with spittle, she stroked an image. Immediately one of the Goodwin children who was pres-

Above: This portrait of Increase Mather is said to be one of the first engraved in America. Below: Clergyman Cotton Mather

ent fell into violent convulsions. Mrs. Glover admitted that she had "a Prince" as her friend and adviser, and later was heard upbraiding the devil for deserting her. She was sentenced to death as a witch.

Mather visited her in jail, where she named confederates who would continue to torment the Goodwin children after she died. Wisely, Mather kept the names a secret. For a while after Mrs. Glover's death, the children were worse. Sometimes they were completely rigid, sometimes limber. "They could fly like geese, and be carried with incredible swiftness through the air, having but just their toes now and then upon the ground, and their arms waved like the wings of a bird."

Fascinated, Mather took one of the girls into his family and started a schedule of prayer to cure her. Eventually the children recovered, partly due, Mather claimed, to the death of a second old woman suspected of witchcraft.

Mather did not believe that the children were acting. Their conduct is striking in some ways, however. They slept well at night. Whenever their parents scolded them, they suffered an immediate seizure. "Whatever work they were bid to do, they would be so snapped in the member which was to do it" that they were unable to move. There seems little doubt that they took some advantage of their situation.

But to dismiss all their conduct as a hoax is to disregard the paralyzing fear of witchcraft that existed at the time. Mrs. Glover, known as a witch, had cursed the Goodwin girl. Doctors had diagnosed her ailments as due to witchcraft. These two circumstances alone were enough in those days to drive a person frantic with fear. The Goodwin children may well have been frightened into hysteria, an emotional disorder that the victim is helpless to control without careful treatment. Convulsive seizures; rigid limbs; a tongue held in unnatural positions; inability to speak; sharp, sudden pain; quick dartings about as if flying; a stiff backward arch of the body—all are possible symptoms of hysteria.

Cotton Mather's wise approach to the Goodwin children no doubt helped their recovery. He gave them his support and reassurance and refused to aggravate matters by accusing the persons Mrs. Glover had named as confederates. He could not help a feeling of elation, however. He had been witness to what he believed was an actual case of witchcraft, proof that the devil could enter even the home of a pious man like John Goodwin. Mather's book *Memorable Providences* was intended to confirm that "the malice of Satan and his instruments is very great against the children of God; that the clearest Gospel-light shining in a place will not keep some from entering into hellish contracts with infernal spirits."

"Go then, my little book," he said in its preface. "Go tell mankind that there are devils and witches. . . . The houses of Christians, where our God has his constant worship, have undergone the annoyance of evil spirits."

Memorable Providences was a sensation. Here was the report of a contemporary event, frightening but exciting, and written by a respected authority. The Goodwin case was the talk of the day. The world of invisible beings had come hauntingly and achingly to life.

"An Evil Hand
Is on Them"

The winter of 1692 was a gray and gloomy time in Massachusetts. The charter was to be replaced by a new one that definitely made Massachusetts a royal colony. It gave power to a royal governor and a popular assembly and granted voting rights based on property ownership, not church membership. The old Bible colony as such was doomed. The frontiers were being attacked by the French of Canada and their Indian allies. The treasury of the colony was almost bankrupt. The people themselves felt deeply uneasy as they wondered what further misfortune might strike them.

When trouble came, it seemed slight at first. In Salem Village (now the town of Danvers), two girls in the family of the Reverend Samuel Parris—his nine-year-old daughter Elizabeth and his eleven-year-old niece Abigail Williams—began to act strangely, staring vacantly into space and suffering peculiar spasms and convulsions. Salem Village was a typical small town of the period—close-knit and gossipy. Whatever happened at the parsonage soon became common talk. Word of the girls' malady spread, and so, it appeared, did the malady itself. Other girls in the village were showing the same symptoms.

Dr. Griggs, the village physician, was called in. When he was unable to discover what was wrong, he gave the diagnosis usual under such circumstances: "An evil hand is on them."

No more fateful words could have been spoken. The girls knew their horrible meaning only too well. The Goodwin case had been thoroughly discussed throughout the colony. The Reverend Mr. Parris owned Cotton Mather's book and other books on witchcraft; the subject must have been talked about in the family and among the neighbors. Close at hand there was also another source of information—the Parrises' two West Indian slaves, Tituba and her husband John Indian. The girls of the household had spent a good deal of time with these servants, both of whom were deeply conscious of magic and the supernatural. The two youngsters had watched Tituba at her palmistry and fortune-telling and had listened to West Indian tales of ghosts and magic as they sat in the warmth of Tituba's domain, the kitchen.

This secret world of spirits and the occult was exciting. The two girls had told their friends of its fascination. Word had quietly spread and Tituba's kitchen had become a gathering place for a number of girls and young women when they could get away from home. All their investigations into Tituba's lore had been carried on stealthily, however. The girls were aware that the knowledge they were gaining was considered evil by the community. They must have talked about it among themselves, but because they were forced to keep it secret it may have become an obsession in their lives. Then, too, they could not help feeling guilty and somewhat fearful—of what, they did not know. Their overexcited, fearful, guiltridden state of mind may have been one of the chief causes of the malady that had attacked them and that had baffled Dr. Griggs.

And now, as if to fulfill their worst fears, a diagnosis had been made: an evil hand was on them; they were bewitched; the devil and his helpers were lurking near, silent and invisible.

The girls were overcome with terror. Samuel Parris, brooding over the situation, probably remembered Cotton Mather's experience with the Goodwin children and his use of prayer in fighting witchcraft. He called the clergymen of the neighboring towns to his home, to observe the girls and to pray with them. By

A "witch house," Salem, Massachusetts

now, their convulsions were worse; at times, also, their bodies were twisted into strange contortions and became rigid; at other times they choked so badly that breathing was difficult; sometimes they shrieked because of sharp pains. The ministers offered their prayers, but to little effect. As they watched the girls' sufferings they agreed that this was a case of witchcraft and that the devil had begun his campaign against New England on a new front.

By now, the whole community was aroused to a sense of danger and threat. If the girls were bewitched, there must be witches in the vicinity. Who were they?

It was a common belief that bewitched persons were able to see their tormentors even if they came as specters invisible to other people. Accordingly, the girls were urged to name the witches. Distracted and frightened, they had no answer to what they did not know. Finally, when community pressure on them failed, a neighboring woman, Mrs. Sibley—a true Puritan busybody—took matters into her own hands. In an old English book she had found a recipe for making the bewitched speak out against their tormentors. Tituba, given the directions, followed them: she baked a cake of rye meal mixed with the girls' urine and fed it to a dog.

Now the girls were more fearful than ever. Magic had been used against them. What would happen if they failed to heed it? When, some time later, Samuel Parris heard of what Mrs. Sibley had done, he was furious. "It is a going to the devil for help against the devil," he said. "The devil has been raised among us and his rage is vehement and terrible."

In this situation the girls could keep silent no longer. They named three women as the witches who were tormenting them: Sarah Good, Sarah Osburn, and Tituba. These three were natural targets for anyone casting about for witches. Sarah Good

Arresting a witch

was a bedraggled, rough-speaking ne'er-do-well who often was homeless and could be seen wandering from door to door with her children, seeking shelter. Sarah Osburn had a respectable enough background, but there had been some scandal concerning her and recently she had given up going to church—the latter a bad sign in itself. Tituba was of another race, a slave, an alien who stood out in the community because she was different.

Warrants for the arrest of the women were issued on February 29, 1692. The three were to appear on March 1 at Samuel Ingersoll's tavern, where the magistrates were to examine them concerning charges that at various times in the past two months they had practiced witchcraft against Elizabeth Parris, Abigail Williams, and two other girls.

The Afflicted Girls

At about this time, Samuel Parris decided to remove his daughter from the uproar now raging in the village. He sent her to stay with friends in another town. There, in calmer surroundings, she recovered and there she stayed until the witchcraft affair was over.

Besides eleven-year-old Abigail Williams, eight other girls and young women afflicted by witches remained in Salem Village. All of them were referred to as the "afflicted girls" or the "afflicted children."

Twelve-year-old Ann Putnam was the daughter of Sergeant Thomas Putnam. Ann's mother—Ann, Sr.—was highstrung, imaginative, and sensitive. Her daughter was like her. The two undoubtedly reacted to each other's emotions, so much so that

Ann Putnam, Sr., soon was drawn into the circle of the afflicted. The Putnams were a socially prominent family with a good deal of influence in the village. Their home became a center for much of the witchcraft excitement, and young Ann took a leading part in it.

One of the persons who shared the Putnams' overwrought emotions was Mercy Lewis, seventeen years old, their servant.

Mary Warren, twenty years old, was a servant in the family of John Procter.

Elizabeth Booth, eighteen, was a village girl whose family lived near the Procters.

Sarah Churchill, twenty, was a servant in the family of George Jacobs, Sr.

Elizabeth Hubbard, seventeen, was a niece of Dr. Griggs's wife and lived with the Griggs family.

Mary Walcott, seventeen, was the daughter of Captain Jonathan Walcott, deacon of the parish.

Susannah Sheldon, eighteen, was the daughter of a village family.

Before the witchcraft affair was ended, these young women were all to play active roles in it.

"Have You Made No Contract with the Devil?"

On the morning of March 1, 1692, Samuel Ingersoll's tavern was surrounded by a throng of people waiting for the magistrates to arrive to question the three suspected witches. Farmers, housewives, children—everyone had left his work undone in order to be present at the most exciting event the people of Salem Village could remember. Little groups stood talking about the three women. Looking back, almost everyone could remember some incident that had seemed unimportant at the time, but that now appeared incriminating.

By the time magistrates John Hathorne and Jonathan Corwin arrived, the crowd had grown too large for the tavern. Accordingly, the meetinghouse was opened and everyone trooped in, looking forward to an interesting day.

Sarah Good was the first to be examined. John Hathorne did most of the questioning. His manner was far from impartial. Plainly he thought the woman guilty and hoped to bully her into a confession.

"Sarah Good," he began, "what evil spirit have you familiarity with?"

"None," she replied.

"Have you made no contract with the devil?"

"No."

"Why do you hurt these children?"

"I do not hurt them. I scorn it."

That might be, Hathorne was thinking, but possibly she had familiars who, as specters, did her wicked work.

"Who do you employ then to do it?" he asked.

"I employ nobody."

"What creature do you employ then?"

"No creature, but I am falsely accused."

Turning to the afflicted girls, Hathorne asked if Sarah Good was one of the persons who had tormented them. They replied that she was. Almost at once they began to have seizures and to cry out about sharp pains.

"Sarah Good," said Hathorne, "do you not see now what you have done? Why do you not tell us the truth? Why do you thus torment these poor children?"

Sarah Good stood firm. She did not torment them, she protested, and added that Sarah Osburn was the guilty person.

The clerk who recorded Sarah Good's examination noted: "Her answers were in a very wicked, spiteful manner, reflecting and retorting against the authority with base and abusive words and many lies. . . . It was said that her husband said that he was afraid that she was either a witch or would be one very quickly."

Sarah Osburn also claimed to be innocent. When she looked at the girls and they were tormented, she refused to take responsibility. Perhaps her specter had caused their suffering, she admitted, but added that possibly the devil might go around in her likeness to afflict people. In other words, perhaps the devil could do his work through the specter of an innocent person who had not made a contract with him. Sarah Osburn had touched on something important. Her idea was ignored at the time, but it was to loom large in the months that followed.

When Tituba's turn came, she at first claimed innocence, but quickly began a long confession.

"The devil came to me and bid me serve him," she said. In return for her allegiance he promised her many fine things. She had signed her mark, "red like blood," in his book. In it were nine other marks, two of them made by Sarah Good and Sarah Osburn.

"Four women sometimes hurt the children. . . . Goody Osburn and Sarah Good, and I do not know who the others were. Sarah Good and Osburn would have me hurt the children, but I would not," Tituba said.

She further testified that the specter of a tall man dressed in black had appeared to her and had threatened harm to her if she did not torment the children.

As her story went on, it grew in richness and variety. The man had once appeared to her and said, "Kill the children." Sometimes his spirit appeared in the form of a hog or a huge black dog, which could change into the man's shape. This man had a yellow bird that stayed with him.

Sarah Good also had a yellow bird as a familiar, Tituba added, and Sarah Osburn had a yellow dog and "a thing with a head like a woman, with two legs, and wings," and another thing, hairy and about two or three feet tall, that walked "upright like a man."

Tituba had also seen the specters of two rats—a red rat and a black rat—who had said to her, "Serve me."

She admitted that her specter had afflicted the children, but she claimed that the man had forced her into this act. She and the other witches rode through the air on sticks and poles to do their witchcraft errands, she said.

As she began speaking the girls were seized with convulsions, but when she started to confess, they quieted. The people of Salem Village listened to her story in fascinated horror. Tituba thoroughly believed in witchcraft. Before her testimony was over, she was having convulsive seizures like those of the girls. She may actually have had hysterical hallucinations and thought parts of her story were true. It may be, too, that, seeing how spellbound her audience was and knowing she was believed guilty anyway, she decided to make her tale as lurid as possible. Its effect was overwhelming. The devil's attack was even more widespread than the people of the village had thought. Tituba had mentioned *nine* marks in the devil's book. Who were the other witches?

The three women were queried further in the five days that followed. They had been arrested specifically for practicing witchcraft against some of the girls, who testified that specters of the accused women had visited them and had tortured them by pinching, pricking, biting, and almost choking them to death. Other testimony not strictly related to the charges was allowed by the magistrates, however.

Any small town of that period, where people knew each other well and had few interests outside the community, was sure to be boiling with spites, grudges, and suspicions. These feelings may have been kept secret over the years, but they were only awaiting a chance to erupt. Now they came out in court. Sarah Good, for instance, sometimes had cursed people for not giving her shelter; soon afterward, various individuals now remembered, their cattle, their sheep, or their hogs had been taken ill or had disappeared. These events were probably pure coincidence and many of them had happened years before, but they were brought up in court as sure proof of witchcraft and were accepted as such by the magistrates.

On March 7, the three women were committed to jail in Boston, to await a further decision on their cases. Sarah Osburn died there two months later, unable to endure the hardships of a seventeenth-century prison.

Another Witch

March 11, 1692, was set aside as a day of fasting and prayer in Salem Village. Samuel Parris consulted with his fellow ministers in Essex County about the still unknown witches who might at any moment attack the town. Already things were in a turmoil. Far from being cured by the jailing of their afflictors, the girls were still being tormented. Tituba's testimony still haunted the people. Their terror might easily change to panic if more witches were uncovered. For a crucial moment, Salem Village stood balanced between sanity and chaos.

Then the balance tipped—toward chaos. On March 11, one of the girls, Ann Putnam, cried out that another witch was afflicting her. When Ann named Martha Corey, the townspeople were appalled. It had been easy to believe that Sarah Good, Sarah Osburn, and Tituba were witches, but Martha Corey was a different kind of person, a greatly respected woman and a devout church member. True, she had attracted more attention to herself than usual during the past few days because of her attitude toward the witchcraft proceedings. Frankly, she thought they were nonsense and said so, expressing doubts as to the sincerity of the afflicted girls. She refused to go to the hearings and tried to prevent her husband, Giles Corey, from going. His complaints about this and the similar complaints of two of her sons-in-law had caused a certain amount of gossip.

Because of Martha Corey's good reputation, the members of the church were unwilling to proceed against her without first talking with her. Accordingly, Edward Putnam and Ezekiel Cheever, church members, went to call on her. First, however, as a means of checking Ann Putnam's story, they stopped to ask her how the specter who was tormenting her was dressed. Ann Putnam's reply was that Martha Corey had blinded her for the moment and she could not see the specter's clothes.

When the two men arrived at Martha Corey's, she showed no surprise. "I know what you are come for," she said. "You are come to talk with me about being a witch, but I am none. I cannot help people's talking of me."

She was told that an afflicted person had complained of her specter and she asked, "But does she tell you what clothes I have on?" When the two men told her Ann Putnam's answer to this question, she smiled, perhaps in grim appreciation of its cleverness.

Her question about the clothes had been sensible, as the clothing of the specters had been discussed at the hearings and she had no doubt heard reports of this. But the two men interpreted her awareness of why they had come, her question, and her smile as signs of a witch's insight. When she declared that she did not think there were any witches, they were indignant and told her they were convinced of the guilt of the other accused women. But, she protested, they were "idle, slothful persons," while she was a good church member. The two men replied that witches had often crept into churches.

The visit of Putnam and Cheever failed to convince the church members of Martha Corey's innocence; after more discussion a warrant was taken out for her arrest. By then, it was March 19, a Saturday, and she was not arrested until Monday.

On that same Saturday, the Reverend Deodat Lawson arrived in the village. He had been Samuel Parris's predecessor and he was to preach the sermon in church the next day. On Saturday evening, Lawson went to pay a call at the Parris home. In his account, *A Brief and True Narrative*, he told what happened.

When I was there, his [Samuel Parris's] kinswoman Abigail Williams (about 12 years of age) had a grievous fit; she was at first hurried with violence to and fro in the room (although Mrs. Ingersoll endeavored to hold her), sometimes making as if she would fly, stretching up her arms as high as she could and crying "Whish, whish, whish!" several times. Presently after, she said, "There is Goodwife Nurse" and said, "Do you not see her? Why, there she stands!" And the said Goodwife N. offered her the Book, but she was resolved she would not sign it, saying, "I won't, I won't, I won't take it. I do not know what Book it is. I am sure it is none of God's Book. It is the Devil's Book, for aught I know." After that, she run to the fire, and begun to throw fire brands about the house; and run against the back, as if she would run up the chimney and, as they said, she had attempted to go into the fire in other fits.

By this time the anxious attention of the whole village was centered on the girls. As young people they had been accustomed to a society where they were "seen and not heard," and they found their new importance a heady thing. Already so frightened and hysterical that they were not wholly responsible for their actions, they were beginning to realize what an awful power they, as bewitched persons, could wield.

Deodat Lawson saw that power in action the next day when he attempted to preach his sermon. Several of the afflicted girls were in church and so was Martha Corey, who felt herself innocent and evidently saw no good reason to stay home. "They [the girls] had several sore fits . . . which did something interrupt me in my First Prayer," Lawson wrote. "After psalm was sung, Abigail Williams said to me, 'Now stand up and name your text.'"

Another of the afflicted persons shouted out, after Lawson began his sermon, "Now there is enough of that." In the middle of the service, Abigail Williams called out, "Look where Goodwife Corey sits on the beam suckling her yellow bird between her fingers." Young Ann Putnam said that there was a yellow bird sitting on Lawson's hat, which hung by the pulpit, but her family kept her from shouting it aloud.

To a community that feared the devil and believed in witchcraft, no better proof of an evil presence could have been given: the most sacred time in the Puritan week, Sunday worship, had been disrupted. Surely the girls would not cause such a commotion unless they were truly bewitched.

On Monday morning the meetinghouse held an expectant crowd when Martha Corey was brought in for questioning. She answered questions with her usual directness. She did not afflict the girls, she said. When she was asked who did, she replied, "I do not know. How should I know?"

"I am a gospel woman," she protested.

"Gospel witch! Gospel witch!" shrieked the girls.

Ann Putnam testified that she had seen the specters of Martha Corey and another woman praying to the devil.

"We must not believe these distracted children," said Martha Corey.

Even as she spoke, the girls appeared to be suffering. When she nervously bit her lips, they screamed that they were being bitten; when she pressed her fingers together, they howled that they were being pinched. One of the girls shouted that she could see the black man whispering in Martha Corey's ear.

One of the Salem girls accusing a witch

[30]

The magistrates could not see anyone biting or pinching the girls, nor could they see the black man, yet the evidence of something evil seemed too strong for them to ignore. Martha Corey was ordered to join the other accused witches in the Boston jail.

Rebecca Nurse

Martha Corey's imprisonment would not end the threat of witches, the people of Salem Village now realized. Word had spread that Deodat Lawson had been present when Goodwife Nurse's specter had appeared to Abigail Williams on Saturday.

To many of the townspeople, Rebecca Nurse seemed an unlikely witch. She was a gentle elderly woman known for her goodness and piety. The matriarch of a large family, she lived surrounded by her children and grandchildren on a huge farm. Her husband had started modestly, but by means of hard work and a good business sense had become an important landowner. Admirable as the Nurses were, some people in the town resented them, partly because they were successful and partly because they kept to themselves. Moreover, the Nurses had taken a doubting attitude toward the bewitched girls and had stayed away from them, showing what many townspeople felt was a less than decent concern for their well-being.

It was no surprise when Rebecca Nurse was brought to the meetinghouse for examination on March 24. The girls were there, twisting and turning and crying out that Rebecca Nurse was tormenting them. Now, too, there was a new complainant, Mrs. Ann Putnam, Sr. Both she and her husband testified that

Mrs. Nurse had tempted Mrs. Putnam to evil and had greatly hurt her. Rebecca Nurse was clearly puzzled by these accusations and protested her innocence. Her manner was so guileless that the magistrates were inclined to believe her. At this point, Ann Putnam, Sr., rose, screaming, "Did you not bring the black man with you; did you not bid me tempt God and die? How oft have you eat and drunk your own damnation?"

"Oh, Lord, help me," moaned Rebecca Nurse, spreading out her hands in supplication.

Her action was the signal for pandemonium. Shrieking and yelping, the girls immediately fell into seizures.

"Do you not see what a solemn condition these are in?" asked Magistrate Hathorne. "When your hands are loose, the persons are afflicted." He went on to remark that she was standing with dry eyes while many in the crowd were crying. (He knew that witches supposedly lacked the ability to weep.)

"You do not know my heart," replied Rebecca Nurse sadly.

"They accuse you of hurting them," said Hathorne, "and if you think it is not unwillingly but by design, you must look upon them as murderers."

"I cannot tell what to think of it," Rebecca Nurse said in bewilderment.

To more charges that her specter had afflicted the girls and Mrs. Putnam, she answered, "I cannot help it. The devil may appear in my shape."

Now the girls were shouting that a black man was whispering in her ear and that birds were flying around her. Whichever way she moved, the girls, acting together, took the same position. But there was worse to come. Rebecca Nurse's specter had appeared to her, Mary Walcott testified, and had said that in the past she had been instrumental in the deaths of several townspeople.

By now the courtroom was in such tumult that the clerk missed part of the testimony. Finally, like those accused before her, Rebecca Nurse was consigned to Boston jail.

In the afternoon of this same day, Deodat Lawson delivered another sermon, this time about the threat that hung over Salem Village. Since his arrival he had seen enough evidence to convince him that the devil was at large.

"Satan is representing his infernal forces; and the devils seem to come armed, mustering amongst us," he warned. "I am this day commanded to call and cry an alarm unto you: arm, arm, arm, handle your arms, see that you are fixed and in readiness, as faithful soldiers under the Captain of our salvation, that, by the shield of faith, ye and we all may resist the fiery darts of the wicked. . . . To our honored magistrates, here present this day to inquire into these things, give me leave, much honored, to offer one word for your consideration. Do all that in you lies to check and rebuke Satan, endeavoring, by all ways and means that are according to the rule of God, to discover his instruments in these horrid operations."

His sermon came at a crucial time. It focused the fears of the villagers and roused them to a mortal war with the devil himself. There was no turning back, they realized; evil must be rooted out. Yet, if his listeners had been less stirred by his militant words, they might have heard more clearly his words of caution. Beware of accusing persons carelessly, Lawson said; the devil may take the shape of an innocent person.

One more supposed witch was arrested that day—five-year-old Dorcas Good, daughter of Sarah Good. Dorcas freely confessed that both she and her mother were witches. The child said that she herself had a snake as a familiar; it sucked blood from between her fingers. She spread her hand and revealed a little red spot like an insect bite. That evidence and her confession were proof enough for the magistrates, and Dorcas was packed off to jail.

"We Shall All Be Devils and Witches"

The events of the past week had followed one another so quickly that there had been little time for quiet thought and for questioning the magistrates' judgment. Fear and suspicion had swept over the village like a wave, and few people had been able to resist it.

Martha Corey stood fast in her refusal to believe in witches, and so did John Procter, a farmer of good reputation. On the morning after the questioning of Mrs. Nurse, he appeared in the village in a rage. He had come, he told a friend, to take home his servant, Mary Warren, one of the afflicted girls. They should all be thrashed, he said. "If they [the girls] are let alone, we shall all be devils and witches quickly," he shouted.

Salem Village was taking its bewitched girls seriously, and in scorning the general opinion John Procter took more risk than he may have realized.

Sarah Cloyse showed her scorn in a quieter but no less decisive way. On Sunday, April 3, she went to church, but only at the urging of her friends. She was Rebecca Nurse's sister and although she believed in witchcraft she knew that her sister was not a witch. She can hardly be blamed if she was not exactly in a mood of Christian charity. Then Samuel Parris announced the Biblical quotation that was to be the text of his sermon: "Have not I chosen you twelve and one of you is a devil?" Whom could Mr. Parris mean but her sister? It was too much for Sarah Cloyse. She walked out of church and slammed the door behind her. In the stillness of the meetinghouse that slam echoed; it continued to echo in the days that followed.

Almost at once the girls began to see the specters of Sarah Cloyse and Elizabeth Procter, wife of John Procter. On April 4 the two women were charged with witchcraft. Warrants for their arrest were issued on April 8.

On April 11, five men from Boston joined the local magistrates to examine Sarah Cloyse and Elizabeth Procter. The new magistrates were James Russell, Isaac Addington, Samuel Appleton, Samuel Sewall, and Deputy Governor Thomas Danforth, who presided.

Sarah Cloyse showed her spunk when John Indian accused her of hurting him.

"When did I hurt thee?" she asked.

"A great many times."

"Oh, you are a grievous liar," said Sarah Cloyse.

Samuel Parris questioned the girls. "Abigail Williams, did you see a company at Mr. Parris's house eat and drink?" he asked. He obviously knew what the answer would be.

Abigail replied that she had seen witches taking the devil's sacrament, or communion, in Mr. Parris's pasture and that Sarah Good and Sarah Cloyse were the deacons who led the others in drinking the "wine like blood."

At this astounding testimony Sarah Cloyse fainted, but she received no sympathy.

"Oh," the girls jeered, "her spirit has gone to prison to her sister Nurse."

The presence of the new magistrates did nothing to quiet the disorder in the room. The audience screamed accusations and the girls moaned and yelped and fell into seizures. Shouting

above the din, John Procter tried to defend his wife. He succeeded only in calling attention to himself and was soon accused
by the girls. The result of the hearings was that Sarah Cloyse,
Elizabeth Procter, and John Procter were committed to jail.

The introduction of the new magistrates from the highest
colonial court, in Boston, had changed the whole witchcraft
affair from a local to a colony-wide one and had increased its
importance. There was little hope now that it would quietly die
down.

On April 18, warrants were issued for the arrest of four
more accused witches or wizards. Three of them were Giles
Corey, husband of Martha Corey, Abigail Hobbs, and Bridget
Bishop. The fourth was a surprise; she was Mary Warren, the
afflicted girl who was the Procters' servant.

Mary Warren had apparently stopped to think a bit. John
Procter's firm stand against witchcraft may have impressed her.
The jailing of the Procters, her employers, may have given her
a final jolt. Presently she was murmuring to those who would
listen that the magistrates might just as well examine Keysar's
daughter, a girl in the village who was known to be insane, as
take notice of what she or any of the afflicted girls said.

"When I was afflicted, I thought I saw the apparitions of a
hundred persons," she admitted. Her head had been "distem-
pered," she said. Now that she was well again, she could not
say she had really seen any of these persons.

Before long, rumors of what Mary Warren was whispering
reached the other girls. Almost at once they accused her of tormenting them and of signing the devil's book.

On April 19, Mary Warren faced her accusers in court. As
she glanced at them they fell into convulsions, moaning and
shrieking.

"You were a little while ago an afflicted person; now you
are an afflicter. How comes this to pass?" asked Samuel Parris.

"I look up to God and take it to be a great mercy of God," answered Mary Warren.

"What, do you take it to be a great mercy to afflict others?" said Samuel Parris.

Now John Indian and a Mrs. Pope, who had joined the afflicted, began to writhe. It was more than Mary Warren could endure. She fell into convulsions. Some of the girls explained that she had been about to confess, but that the specters of Martha Corey and the Procters had struck her down so that she would tell nothing.

Presently Mary Warren started up and said, "I will speak. Oh, I am sorry for it," but another convulsion overwhelmed her. Coming to consciousness again, she cried, "I will tell. They did, they did," then fell into a violent spasm. Finally her agony was so great that she was taken from the courtroom.

For the next three weeks she was kept in jail; from time to time the magistrates questioned her. Again and again she denied what she might have said during her seizures, but the magistrates were interested only in a confession of her covenant with the devil. At last, hounded by the magistrates and wracked with convulsions, she confessed to witchcraft and thoroughly implicated the Procters and several other persons. After this, she was released. Quietly she rejoined the ranks of the afflicted and expressed no more doubts about witches.

Giles Corey, Abigail Hobbs, and Bridget Bishop were also examined on April 19. Giles Corey and Bridget Bishop claimed innocence, but the magistrates could see that the girls were tormented at a look from them and cured by their touch.

Some time before, Abigail Hobbs had boasted that she "had sold herself body and soul to the old boy [the devil]." Now she confessed to a great variety of witchcraft and said that she had

Another witch is taken off to jail.

[39]

been at the witches' meeting in Mr. Parris's pasture and had eaten the red bread and drunk the red wine.

All the accused were sent to jail.

In her confession, Abigail Hobbs had named nine persons. On April 21, warrants were served for their arrest. Among them were William and Deliverance Hobbs, parents of Abigail; Mary Esty, sister of Rebecca Nurse and Sarah Cloyse; and Susanna Martin.

The tumult of her examination was too much for poor Deliverance Hobbs. When the girls were seized with convulsions at a look from her and when the accusations started flying, she began to doubt herself. To her, the evidence seemed convincing; perhaps she really had done the things she was accused of. In the end she admitted many acts of witchcraft, naming other guilty persons as well. (Anyone who had attended the court examinations knew the main qualifications for being a good witch, and only a little imagination was needed to make a convincing confession, as many persons were to discover before the summer was over.)

William Hobbs looked on in disgust. When he was examined he proudly maintained his innocence, but was committed to jail.

Mary Esty faced the magistrates with such calm and courtesy that for once they found themselves doubting the girls. "Are you sure?" they asked. Eventually, however, the evidence convinced them and Mary Esty was sent to jail.

At her examination, Susanna Martin, unlike Mary Esty, showed her impatience with what she considered foolishness. She laughed at the girls and said she did not think they were bewitched. "They may lie, for aught I know," she added. Even when she was committed to jail she remained unimpressed. "A false tongue will never make a guilty person," she said.

In prison, Mary Esty continued to conduct herself so well that the jailer, too, had doubts. Soon she was released. She returned home, but three days later Mercy Lewis was seized with such terrible convulsions that the neighbors attending her feared for her life. She moaned the name of Mary Esty. Some of the other girls were sent for, to see whose specter was tormenting Mercy. They agreed that it was Mary Esty's, and she was at once returned to jail.

By now, a sinister rumor was spreading through the town: a clergyman was among the witches. On April 20, young Ann Putnam had been visited by a specter and had cried out, "Oh, dreadful, dreadful, here is a minister come. Whence come you and what is your name? For I will complain of you, even though you are a minister." He had tortured her and almost choked her and had tempted her to write in the devil's book. Finally he had told her his name: George Burroughs.

It was a name she had surely heard, although she had never seen the man. At one time her mother's brother-in-law had been minister in the village, but there had been a dispute about him between two factions of the church and he had been dismissed. George Burroughs had taken his place. Ann's mother and father had always disliked Burroughs because they felt he had deprived their relative of his position.

Burroughs' life in the village had not been happy. He had trouble collecting his salary; many people had been unfriendly; and finally his wife had died. Some years before 1692, he had left the town to go as minister to Wells, Maine. There he had married his third wife. His servant, Mercy Lewis, had stayed behind in the village as servant to the Putnams.

Now young Ann Putnam was whispering that the ghosts of two women had appeared to her and told her that George Burroughs had murdered them. They were Burroughs' first two

wives, both dead for some years. Later, other ghosts appeared to Ann, accusing Burroughs of their murder.

A warrant was sent to Maine, and Burroughs was brought back to the village. He appeared at a public examination on May 9. Because he was a minister, he was first questioned privately by a group of magistrates and clergymen. They found him woefully lax in religious matters. This lack of true Puritan zeal no doubt influenced those who were to judge him.

At his examination, Ann Putnam told her story once again, and Mercy Lewis testified: "Mr. Burroughs carried me up to an exceeding high mountain and showed me all the kingdoms of the earth and told me he would give them all to me if I would write in his book." She had refused.

The girls went on to accuse Burroughs of being the leader of the witches' meetings. He blew a trumpet to summon the witches to Mr. Parris's pasture, they said. The trumpet could be heard for miles, but only by witches. Deliverance Hobbs verified the girls' story and said that she had been at meetings where Burroughs had urged the witches to bewitch the whole town, but to do it gradually. He had taken charge of the devil's sacrament, serving red bread and wine like blood.

Other witnesses declared that Burroughs, though a slightly built man, had always shown strength that could only be superhuman.

In the face of all this testimony, the magistrates decided that jail was the place for him.

A supposed witch, shown here with her black cat,
is shunned and feared by the townspeople.

The Witch
Trials Begin

On May 14, 1692, Sir William Phips, the new royal governor, arrived to take office. He had not expected to face a witchcraft crisis, but he saw that something had to be done at once. The accused witches were in jail awaiting a decision on their fate, and the colony was in an uproar.

Phips appointed a court of judges to try the witches and to reach a final verdict on their cases, allowing no appeal. William Stoughton of Dorchester, the new deputy governor, was made chief justice of the court. Also serving on it were Wait Winthrop, Peter Sergeant, John Richards, and Samuel Sewall, all of Boston, Bartholemew Gedney of Salem, and Nathaniel Saltonstall of Haverhill.

Once the court was established, Phips was satisfied that the witchcraft affair would be settled and he left Boston to take charge of frontier military operations against the French and Indians.

The court opened during the first week in June, 1692. Bridget Bishop was the first defendant to be tried. She had no lawyer, nor did any of the later defendants. The judges, by custom, were expected to protect the rights of the accused, but this part of their duties was slighted. The defendants received no more consideration than they had in the preliminary examinations. The girls writhed and moaned; testimony was admitted whether or not it had any bearing on the actual charges against the accused; the audience shouted comments as they pleased; there was a general air of disorder and a general feeling that the defendants were guilty.

Bridget Bishop was a loud, easygoing woman who had long

been rumored to be a witch; even her husband accused her. Some workmen testified that, some years before, in tearing down a wall of her house, they had come upon a few small images stuck with pins. It may be that she actually had practiced witchcraft. In any case, the twelve-man jury found her guilty, and on June 10 she was hanged on Gallows Hill in Salem, the first of the accused witches to die.

After this first execution the judges took a recess while they considered how to proceed. Several questions were troubling them. In large part, the accused witches had been jailed after their examinations because of the girls' testimony that the witches' specters had tortured them. One of the pieces of evidence used again and again in the examinations had been the torment of the afflicted girls in court by specters after a look from the supposed witch, and the healing of the afflicted at the touch of her hand. Specters were invisible to all but bewitched persons. While the girls' agonies were apparent, was so-called spectral evidence enough to condemn a person? And might not the devil, for his own ends, take the shape of an innocent person, as some of the accused had suggested?

Other evidence against some of the accused had seemed to result from their own ill temper. They had scolded and threatened their neighbors and had been held responsible for any ensuing ill fortune the neighbors might suffer.

The world of witchcraft was largely an invisible one. In a drama of shifting specters and spirits, what evidence should the court consider "real"? How much importance should spectral evidence be given? Should the "look and touch" method be used to identify a witch? Just how could the court prove that a person was a witch? How could the innocent be protected?

Even before the court opened, John Richards, one of the judges, had asked Cotton Mather's advice on proper trial procedure. Mather had replied with a thoughtful letter.

I must most humbly beg you that . . . you do not lay more stress upon pure specter testimony than it will bear. . . . It is very certain that the devils have sometimes represented the shapes of persons not only innocent but also very virtuous. . . . Moreover, I do suspect that persons who have too much indulged themselves in malignant, envious, malicious ebullitions of their souls may unhappily expose themselves to the judgment of being represented by devils, of whom they never had any vision, and with whom they have much less written a covenant.

Now first a credible confession of the guilty witches is one of the most hopeful ways of coming at them, and I say a credible confession because even confession itself sometimes is not credible.

He ended his letter with a suggestion that for some witches there might be a penalty less than death.

On June 15, 1692, at the request of the judges, several eminent Massachusetts clergymen wrote their recommendations. They were much like Cotton Mather's: treat the accused tenderly, with "as little as is possible of such noise, company, and openness as may too hastily expose them"; require more than spectral evidence; do not consider "look and touch" evidence an infallible sign of guilt. The clergymen ended the letter, nevertheless, by calling for "the speedy and vigorous prosecution of such as have rendered themselves obnoxious, according to the direction given in the laws of God, and the wholesome statutes of the English nation, for the detection of witchcraft."

An argument among the judges about the use of spectral evidence seems to have followed. In dissatisfaction, Nathaniel Saltonstall resigned from the court; Jonathan Corwin took his place. William Stoughton was particularly insistent that spectral evidence should be allowed; he firmly believed that the devil could appear only in the shape of a guilty person, never an innocent one. His position as chief justice probably gave weight to his opinion. When the trials were resumed late in June, spectral evidence was accepted.

On June 29, Sarah Good, Sarah Wilds, Elizabeth How, Susanna Martin, and Rebecca Nurse were sentenced to be hanged as witches.

In the trial of Rebecca Nurse, there had been testimony by the girls and new testimony by Ann Putnam, Sr., that more ghosts had accused Mrs. Nurse of murder, but a man named John Tarbell testified that, back in the spring, the girls had at first seen only the specter of a pale woman. They had not accused Rebecca Nurse until her name was suggested to them either by Ann Putnam, Sr., or by Mercy Lewis. He was not sure which.

Rebecca Nurse impressed the jury as innocent and they gave the verdict "Not guilty." At once the courtroom broke into bedlam as the girls howled and writhed in torment.

One of the witnesses against Rebecca Nurse had been Deliverance Hobbs. Startled that an imprisoned person should be used to testify against her and questioning the legality of such a procedure, Mrs. Nurse had exclaimed, "What, do you bring her? She is one of us." William Stoughton had interpreted this remark as one witch's recognition of another. Upon hearing the verdict, he asked the jury if they had carefully considered Mrs. Nurse's words. They decided to consult again and to ask the defendant what she had meant.

Rebecca Nurse was old and rather deaf. Worn out by her stay in prison and by the confusion in the courtroom, she did not hear the questioning juryman who came to her nor, looking straight ahead, did she even see him. Her silence was proof enough for the jury; they changed their verdict to "Guilty."

The Nurse family immediately took her case to Governor

Phips, who had come back to Boston briefly. He agreed to a reprieve for her, but when the girls were tormented anew by her specter she was again condemned to die. On July 19, she and the others sentenced to death on June 29 were hanged. Sarah Good remained spiteful to the end. When, at the gallows, the Reverend Nicholas Noyes told her she was a witch and knew it, she replied: "You are a liar. I am no more a witch than you are a wizard, and if you take away my life, God will give you blood to drink." Those persons with long memories thought of her words years later when Noyes, desperately ill, choked of a hemorrhage in his throat and died.

More and More Witches

Jailings and executions had not made the number of witches around Salem Village any fewer. On the contrary, new witches were being discovered every day, and the witchcraft epidemic was spreading.

A woman in Andover, a neighboring town, had been ill with a fever for a long time. When her doctor was of no help, her husband, Joseph Ballard, persuaded young Ann Putnam and Mary Walcott to come to Andover to find out who was bewitching his wife. The girls were received with awe and reverence, and at a gathering in the meetinghouse the Reverend Mr. Barnard offered prayer for their success. They were then solemnly escorted to the Ballard home. They named several persons who, they said, were tormenting Mrs. Ballard. Before the resulting witchcraft panic died down in Andover, almost fifty persons had been jailed.

By now, people were beginning to realize that the surest way to avoid being accused was to be an accuser. As a result, more and more people were crying "Witch, witch" against their neighbors. The accused persons, in turn, were beginning to see that the surest way to avoid death was to confess to witchcraft. A witch who confessed did not end up on the gallows. Only those who stubbornly maintained their innocence were executed. Accordingly, many accused persons, nagged by their relatives to confess to anything in order to save their lives, gave colorful accounts of their careers as witches. More often than not, urged on by the authorities, they ended by accusing other persons.

Some accused persons, unwilling to confess to what they had not done, were subjected to endless questioning and even to torture by law officers. Finally, many of them confessed out of sheer exhaustion and a pitiful longing merely to be let alone.

There were also some persons who were confused by the constant alarms and excitement. They became unable any longer to see a difference between a real and a spirit world, and actually believed themselves to be witches.

As he watched the prison fill and as he heard the tales of the newcomers, John Procter was more than ever convinced that a terrible wrong was being done. On July 23, he wrote a letter to the Boston clergymen on behalf of himself and his fellow prisoners. Many of the confessions and accusations were lies, Procter said, and had been made only after arrested persons were tied neck and heels together until the blood gushed out at their noses. The accusers, the judges, and the jury had already condemned him and his fellow prisoners before they had been tried, Procter wrote. He begged that the trials be moved to Boston or that the judges be changed, and asked that some of the clergymen attend the court sessions in order that "thereby you may be the means of saving the shedding of our innocent blood."

Procter's letter had little effect. On August 5, he and Elizabeth Procter, George Burroughs, George Jacobs, Sr., John Willard, and Martha Carrier were brought to trial.

Over thirty people from the town of Ipswich, his former home, had signed a petition to the judges, testifying to John Procter's good character, and over twenty of the Procters' neighbors in Salem Village also petitioned for them. In acting for the Procters, these people risked accusations of witchcraft against themselves, but their courage gained nothing. The jury found John and Elizabeth Procter guilty.

George Burroughs did not help his cause when he offered the jury a paper he claimed to have written, denying that there were witches who could torment victims by specters. In the past he had often declared that witches existed. It was later discovered that he had copied the paper from an English book, *A Candle in the Dark*, by Thomas Ady. Against the girls' flood of testimony, Burroughs was helpless.

Margaret Jacobs, granddaughter of George Jacobs, Sr., had been arrested by law officers. Threatened with the dungeon and hanging, she had confessed to witchcraft and had implicated her grandfather and Burroughs. Her conscience gave her no ease, however, and in a pathetic attempt to set the record straight she told the court of the pressure to make her confess and admitted that her statements had been altogether "false and untrue." Her pleas failed to save Burroughs and Jacobs.

All the defendants were sentenced to be hanged. Only Elizabeth Procter was reprieved, because she was expecting a child, who was considered innocent and therefore not subject to death.

Facing the people assembled for the hangings on August 19, the condemned persons were calm and dignified. George Burroughs stood on the ladder to the gallows and spoke sincerely of his innocence; he ended with the Lord's Prayer, which no witch or wizard was supposed to be capable of repeating. A murmur of protest against his death ran through the crowd. It was silenced only when Cotton Mather rode forward on horseback to assure the people that Burroughs had not been a properly ordained minister and was genuinely guilty.

Growing Doubts

The murmur of protest among the crowd on Gallows Hill was one small sign that public opinion about the bewitchments was changing.

On August 9, Robert Pike of Salisbury had written a letter to Judge Jonathan Corwin. Pike, himself a magistrate, seriously questioned the testimony of the afflicted girls and also doubted the use of the "look and touch" method of determining who was a witch. Far from working through the witches, the devil was working through the afflicted persons, Pike claimed; by their seizures they were being forced to accuse the innocent. The devil had possessed the afflicted persons and the confessing witches and was telling his lies through them. "But if their testimonies be allowed of, to make innocent persons guilty by, the lives of innocent persons are alike in danger of them," he said. As for the "look and touch" evidence used in court, Pike declared that it did not make sense that any person accused of being a witch would perform acts of witchcraft in the courtroom.

Again Cotton Mather warned against condemning persons solely on spectral evidence and the look and touch of a supposed witch. If there was uncertainty about accused persons, it might be better to reprieve or to exile them, he said.

The court met twice in September and condemned fifteen persons to death. Of these, eight were executed on September 22. They were Martha Corey, Mary Esty, Alice Parker, Ann Pudeator, Margaret Scott, Wilmot Reed, Samuel Wardwell, and Mary Parker.

Mary Esty and her sister Sarah Cloyse had earlier requested the judges to act as counsel for them, to advise them when necessary, and had also asked that witnesses in their favor be called. The judges ignored their request. After Mary Esty's conviction by the jury, she petitioned the governor, the judges, and the clergymen of Massachusetts. "By my own innocency I know you are wrong," she wrote. She asked that the authorities examine the afflicted persons and the accusing confessors very strictly in order to determine the truth, and begged "not for my own life, for I know I must die . . . but if it be possible, that no more innocent blood be shed, which cannot be avoided in the way and course you go in."

There was one more death in September. Giles Corey had been called before the court to answer charges of witchcraft. Although he had originally been swept along by the witchcraft mania, his realization of his own innocence and that of his wife and a summer of observing the accused witches in jail had changed his opinion.

He knew that if he pleaded innocent he would be condemned anyway, and his pride prevented him from joining the ranks of the confessors. He alone among the defendants did not plead guilty or not guilty, but stood mute, refusing to answer any questions in court. He was a stubborn man; nothing could make him speak and so he could not be tried. But he well knew what the penalty for his action would be. His defiance of the court received the punishment prescribed by law. He was stretched on the ground, and weights were piled on him ever increasingly until he was pressed to death. He lived for two

An accused wizard goes to his death.

days under this torture; during this time he remained steadfast. His firmness and dignity made a strong impression on those villagers who were already becoming doubtful about the summer's events.

By his action, Giles Corey also did something for his children. Once witches or wizards were condemned by a jury, their property was seized by the government. But Corey had not been condemned. Before he died he made a legal will that ensured his heirs of their inheritance.

The End
of the Trials

After the executions of September 22, the court adjourned, expecting to meet later in the fall.

By October, public opinion against the trials had spread. Increase Mather had written a paper, *Cases of Conscience concerning Evil Spirits Personating Men*. In it he opposed the use of spectral evidence in court and questioned the testimony of confessed witches against others. He condemned "look and touch" evidence, saying that it was a use of witchcraft. "We ought not to practice witchcraft to discover witches," he said, and added that it was better that ten suspected witches should escape punishment than that one innocent person should be condemned. Mather read his paper to a meeting of Massachusetts clergymen on October 3, 1692.

On October 8 another resident of Boston, Thomas Brattle, wrote a letter and circulated it among his friends. He protested against accepting the testimony of the afflicted girls and the accusing confessors without questioning it. The girls were deluded by the devil, he said, and the devil's book, the witches' meetings, and the mock sacraments were mere fancies of theirs. As for the confessors, he claimed that some of them were known to be crazy and others had been forced into false confessions. He pointed out that some had soon denied their confessions. He also deplored the court's use of evidence that had nothing to do with the original charges against the accused persons.

Sir William Phips had returned from the frontier to find that his court had failed to solve the witchcraft problem. The jails were crowded with indicted persons awaiting trial; more witches were being accused every day; the afflicted persons seemed in worse agony than ever. Many persons, hearing that they were about to be accused, had fled the colony. Accusations were being made against prominent persons whose innocence was beyond doubt. The citizens, distracted by the continuous disturbance, had neglected their farms and businesses throughout the summer. Massachusetts was in an economic slump.

Phips forbade that any more accused persons be committed to jail unless absolutely necessary and wrote to England on October 12 for advice on what to do.

On October 18 he received a letter, not from England but from a group of Andover citizens who asked clemency for the Andover women who had confessed. They had made their confessions out of fear, the letter stated. The witchcraft troubles were likely to continue unless new procedures were adopted, these people warned. "We know not who can think himself safe if the accusations of children and others who are under a diabolical influence shall be received against persons of good fame."

The court that had been appointed in May never met again. In a new approach, Phips and the legislative assembly ordered the Superior Court of Judicature to hold special sessions to try the persons waiting in jail. William Stoughton remained chief justice. The other judges were Samuel Sewall, John Richards, Wait Winthrop, and Thomas Danforth. They started sessions in January, 1693.

The judges agreed that procedures at the Salem trials had been faulty. In the new court, spectral evidence was not given any importance. Without it, most of the cases against accused witches could not be proved. Of the fifty-two persons tried, only three were convicted. All three were confessors. Stoughton signed their death warrants and those of five persons who had previously been condemned. When the king's attorney-general expressed the opinion that evidence against the condemned was no more damaging than against those who had been acquitted, Phips ordered the condemned persons reprieved.

Phips still could get no definite answer to his problems from England, and finally, in May, 1693, he began to clear the jails by discharging the one hundred and fifty witchcraft prisoners who remained. He also issued a general pardon that included those persons who had fled the colony.

Clearing the jails took some time because, as was customary in Massachusetts at the time, the prisoners were not allowed to go free until they had paid for their food and for all the other expenses of their jail terms. They even paid the cost of making the iron chains that had bound their wrists and ankles. Many of the prisoners came from poor families who had great difficulty in raising the money for their release; some of these families never recovered from the financial strain they suffered in this effort. One woman was released only when she went as an indentured servant to a man who paid her prison debts, and Tituba was sold as a slave to a new master when Samuel Parris refused to redeem her. The property of the prisoners had been seized when they were jailed; a great number of them lived out their days in poverty.

Aftermath

In Salem Village the townspeople began to put together the broken fragments of their lives. In the storm of accusations during the past year, neighbor had been pitted against neighbor and almost unforgivable things had been said. Many people had left the village, never to return. The wounds of the witchcraft trouble would take years to heal.

The afflicted girls had been silent since opinion had changed; gradually they faded from public notice. The members of the church felt that Samuel Parris had been at fault in encouraging the girls to name the persons who were afflicting them. Many of the church people had lost friends and relatives among the executed persons and they joined in driving Parris from the town. After a long struggle over money due him, he was finally dismissed in 1697. The shadow of the witchcraft affair hung over him for the rest of his life as he journeyed unhappily from one ministry to another. The Reverend Joseph Green, who succeeded him in Salem Village, worked mightily to erase the enmities caused by the events of 1692.

As the witchcraft fever died down, the people of Massachusetts saw the affair for what it was—a delusion brought on by fear and overexcitement. Great wrong had been done to innocent persons, and no one was without blame. The Massachusetts General Court set aside January 14, 1697, as a day of fasting when the people would ask God's forgiveness for what they had done in 1692. On that day Samuel Sewall, one of the judges in the witchcraft trials, gave his minister a letter to be read aloud from the pulpit. Sewall stood as the clergyman read the letter in which the judge admitted his error against the persons convicted in the trials and asked forgiveness.

On that same day, the jury of the Salem trials also publicly acknowledged their error. For want of knowledge of their own and good advice from others, they had acted on evidence that was not enough to condemn the accused persons to death, the jury said. They spoke of their sorrow and asked forgiveness, saying they had been "under the power of a strong and general delusion."

Of all the persons who had a part in judging the cases, only William Stoughton never expressed remorse. One of the outstanding features of the Salem Village affair is the courage and honesty of many of the participants in publicly admitting that they were wrong. Their action is almost unparalleled in the history of witchcraft.

Of the afflicted girls, only Ann Putnam made public confession of error. In 1706, she asked to be admitted to membership in the Salem Village church and stood quietly while Joseph Green read her statement from the pulpit.

> . . . that I, being in my childhood . . . should be made an instrument for the accusing of several persons of a grievous crime, whereby their lives were taken from them, whom now I have just grounds and good reason to believe they were innocent persons. . . . What was said or done by me against any person I can truly and uprightly say before God and man, I did it not out of anger, malice, or ill will . . . but what I did was ignorantly, being deluded by Satan. I . . . earnestly beg forgiveness of all those unto whom I have given just cause for sorrow and offense, whose relations were taken away and accused.

It is to the everlasting credit of the Reverend Joseph Green and his congregation that they received Ann Putnam forgivingly into their number.

There were still some wrongs to be righted. The jail sentences of the accused witches stood on the public record and their relatives wished their names to be cleared. In 1703, the Massachusetts General Court had declared the witchcraft trials of 1692 unlawful and had disallowed the use of spectral evidence. Still the names of the jailed persons had not been taken from the record. As time went on, a movement also grew to allow their families some financial compensation for their suffering. In 1711, the General Court authorized payments to the families of the executed persons and the condemned persons who had not been executed, although the payments were small and unfairly allotted. Gradually, too, the verdicts against the accused were reversed so that for the most part their reputations were cleared.

Why Did
It Happen?

How shall we judge the Salem witchcraft delusion? Was it, as some historians have claimed, a vengeful plot and a hoax carried out deliberately by the girls with the encouragement of Samuel Parris and some other adults?

Malice against some persons did play a part, and Samuel Parris apparently made no great effort to halt the affair in its early stages. Caution and wisdom such as Cotton Mather had shown in dealing with the Goodwin children were not to be found in a person like Parris. He had a love of excitement; the witchcraft accusations were bound to appeal to his sense of drama.

It is impossible to judge the affair from a twentieth-century point of view. The citizens of seventeenth-century Salem Village thoroughly believed in witchcraft. At the time, they were going through a period of uneasiness and uncertainty. When word spread that the girls were bewitched, fear swept through the community. That fear was heightened by the testimony of Tituba at the first examination.

The terror abroad in the community affected the girls and made them more fearful. From then on, events kindled deepening excitement until mob hysteria resulted. In such a state of public emotion, almost anything becomes believable; irrational acts appear reasonable; the ability to judge objectively is lost; all sense of personal responsibility disappears. Most of the persons who might have had doubts did not dispute the popular viewpoint out of fear for their lives. Even the judges, who should have acted responsibly, were swayed by questionable testimony against the accused. There was, as the jury later stated, "a strong and general delusion."

As for the girls, their very real suffering cannot be described simply as a hoax. They apparently were caught in the grip of hysterical fear. At first, feeling their importance and not understanding how serious the matter was, they seem to have done some play-acting. Before long, however, they were placed in a position where the whole town watched their every word and act and prompted them when they faltered. There was no escape. They collapsed under the weight of public fear. Caught by a force beyond their control, they became ever more hysterical and irresponsible, believing their own imaginings. Mary Warren, as we have seen, tried to break out of the circle of the bewitched and found it impossible to do so. Twice when Mercy Lewis, in hysterical seizures, accused people, she had no recollection of her words when she recovered. She denied the truth of what she had said during her seizures, but the adults who were present would

George Jacobs being accused in Salem

not listen to her. Sarah Churchill privately took back her accusation of George Jacobs, Sr., but said that she had gone too far in the affair to make a public denial and that her minister, Nicholas Noyes, would not believe her, anyway.

The adults surrounding the girls were not above suggesting names of supposed witches to them, and it is only natural that they were the names of persons who had displeased them in some way. Grudges, spites, and jealousies inevitably played their part, but it is a mistake to regard the witchcraft affair as planned. Throughout the summer of 1692, it spread far beyond Salem Village as the number of accusers and confessors multiplied. No one could have at first foreseen that by autumn twenty persons would have been killed and over one hundred and fifty imprisoned, while fifty-five confessed to being witches and countless numbers fled the colony or escaped from jail.

In the face of such madness, it is all the more remarkable that so many persons should later have publicly admitted their error. Through their brave act the Salem witchcraft delusion became a landmark on the road to enlightenment. Although witchcraft trials did not cease immediately in England and Europe, Salem marked the beginning of the end for such events.

Witch-hunting still goes on in other forms, however. Even today, groups of people are made to suffer for their beliefs. Perhaps one of the lessons of the Salem witchcraft delusion is that the opinion of the majority can be wrong. Perhaps we should remember the clear-eyed, stouthearted few at Salem Village— John Procter and Martha Corey and Mary Esty—and listen always for the solitary voices that speak out against the crowd in defense of what they believe. They just might be right.

A Selected Bibliography

Burr, George Lincoln, ed. *Narratives of the Witchcraft Cases, 1648–1706.* (Original Narratives of Early American History, vol. 4). New York: Charles Scribner's Sons, 1914.

Drake, Samuel Gordon. *Annals of Witchcraft in New England and Elsewhere in the United States from Their First Settlement.* (Woodward's Historical Series, No. VIII). Boston: W. Eliot Woodward, 1869.

Hansen, Chadwick. *Witchcraft in Salem.* New York: George Braziller, Inc., 1969.

Kittredge, George Lyman. *Witchcraft in Old and New England.* Cambridge, Mass.: Harvard University Press, 1929.

Levin, David. *What Happened in Salem?* Second ed. New York: Harcourt Brace Jovanovich, Inc., 1960.

Phillips, James Duncan. *Salem in the Seventeenth Century.* Boston: Houghton Mifflin Company, 1933.

Records of Salem Witchcraft Copied from the Original Documents. Roxbury, Mass.: Privately printed for W. Eliot Woodward, 1864.

Schneider, Herbert Wallace. *The Puritan Mind.* (Studies in Religion and Culture, American Religion Series I). New York: Henry Holt and Company, 1930.

Upham, Charles W. *Salem Witchcraft, with an Account of Salem Village and a History of Opinions on Witchcraft and Kindred Subjects.* 2 vols. New York: Frederick Ungar Publishing Co., 1959.

About the Author

ALICE DICKINSON grew up in Massachusetts and is familiar with the area concerning the Salem witchcraft trials. Now a resident of New York City, Ms. Dickinson has been a teacher, a librarian, and an editor with a New York publishing house. She is the author of a number of books for children, all published by Franklin Watts, including *The Sacco-Vanzetti Case, The Boston Massacre, The Stamp Act* (all Focus books), *Charles Darwin and Natural Selection, Carl Linnaeus: Pioneer of Modern Botany, The First Book of Prehistoric Animals, The First Book of Plants,* and *The First Book of Stone Age Man.*

Index

R